A *Shimmer* *of* *Butterflies*

THE BRIEF, BRILLIANT LIFE OF A MAGICAL INSECT

BY JONI PHELPS HUNT

LONDON TOWN PRESS

Jean-Michel Cousteau *presents*
Publishing Director
Jean-Michel Cousteau

A Shimmer of Butterflies
Principal photographers
Robert and Linda Mitchell

Additional photographers
Stanley Breeden; D. Cavagnaro; Hal Clason; Michael Fodgen;
Jeff Foott; John Gerlach; Richard R. Hansen; Martha Hill; Alex
Kerstitch; Frans Lanting; Jeanette Sainz; Kjell B. Sandved;
Kevin Schafer; Larry Ulrich; Larry West; Belinda Wright

London Town Press
2026 Hilldale Drive
La Canada Flintridge, California 91011
www.LondonTownPress.com

Book design by Christy Hale
10 9 8 7 6 5 4 3 2

Printed in Malaysia
Distributed by Publishers Group West/Perseus

Publisher's Cataloging-in-Publication Data
Hunt, Joni Phelps.
A shimmer of butterflies : the brief, brilliant life of a magical
insect / Joni Phelps Hunt ; photographs by Robert and Linda
Mitchell. —2nd ed.
p.   cm. — (London Town wild life series)
Originally published: San Luis Obispo, CA : Blake Books
©1993
Summary: Explores the physical characteristics, life cycles,
behavior, and migratory habits of butterflies and moths
through full-color photographs and text.
Includes bibliographic references and index.
ISBN 0-9666490-6-0
1. Butterflies—Juvenile literature.   2. Moths—Juvenile literature.
[1. Butterflies. 2. Moths.] I. Mitchell, Robert. II. Mitchell,
Linda. III. Title. IV. Series.
QL544.2 H863 2005
595.789—dc22
2004117677

FRONT COVER: A western tiger swallowtail drinks nectar from a
red columbine.

TITLE PAGE: A coral hairstreak butterfly in the Midwest heads
for nectar. The thin thread between its two striped antennae is
the proboscis, or feeding tube, it uses to drink.

HABITAT SHOWCASE: A meadow (pp. 4-5), West Indies rainforest
(pp. 12-13), and North American temperate forest (pp. 26-27)
provide ideal homes for different kinds of butterflies.

BACK COVER: Caterpillars defend themselves in many ways.
Besides having prickly spines, this larva of the Io moth is
toxic. It is found in the Panama rainforest.

Contents

Charisma in living color

As it flutters by, the butterfly charms us with its colors, its grace, the unhurried way it flirts with flowers. But its life isn't as carefree as it looks. Butterflies have deadlines. In the few short weeks or months they have to live, they must meet, mate, produce young, and help ensure that other species reproduce, too.

All the while they must remain on guard against hungry admirers who are intent on making their lives even shorter. And

◄Swallowtail butterflies have distinctive "tails" at wing's end. With strong legs, they hold onto flowers and flutter their wings while fueling up on nectar.

millions of them must live long enough to travel thousands of miles in mass migrations.

Butterflies and their closest relatives, moths, work hard, earning their place on earth as important pollinators. Without them, many flowers and plants could not reproduce.

These two fliers belong to the most successful group of living things on earth: insects. Butterflies and moths differ from other insects in two ways. First is their hollow tongue—a tube, really—called the

▲ In spring, a meadow rich with California poppies, purple lupine, and red owl's clover offers a nectar feast for butterflies.

proboscis. It serves as a straw, letting butterflies and moths get every drop of nectar. Second, their wings display color and pattern in a special way. Like pixel dots on a television screen, millions of tiny scales blend to create each butterfly wing. These soft scales overlap each other like the scales on a lizard's hide.

Scientists call their family *Lepidoptera,* meaning "scaly wing." Scientists who study them are known as Lepidopterists.

Moths have been around for more than 140 million years. Butterflies evolved some 40 million years ago. During their long stay on earth, these creatures have settled almost everywhere. Today, more than

►Butterfly wings are miniature masterpieces of art. Not all are small, either. For its beauty and size, this Cairns birdwing has long been sought after by collectors. Demand for birdwings prompted Australia to protect this native species.

250,000 species of moths and butterflies grace nearly all the earth, except for Antarctica. They live in woodlands, prairies, deserts, meadows, swamps, and tropical rainforests. They thrive on islands, arctic tundra, mountains—even inside ants' nests.

Their size varies, too. The pygmy blue, world's smallest butterfly, has a wingspan of half an inch. This hardy insect can be found on mountain peaks as high as 6,000 feet to the desert floor of Death Valley, California, 178 feet below sea level. The island of Papua New Guinea boasts the world's largest butterfly, a foot-long beauty called the Queen Alexandra birdwing. Both the atlas moth of Asia and the ghost moth of South America are almost as big, with nearly 12-inch wingspans.

◄Watching this common Mormon butterfly feed, it's easy to find its compound eyes and long thin proboscis.

From a scientific standpoint, butterflies and moths aren't that different. Most moths fly by night, rest with their wings flat, and have antennae that are feathery or straight. Most butterflies are active in the day, rest with their wings upright over their backs, and have antennae with knobs on the tips. For the most part, though, butterflies and moths are more alike than different.

Like other insects, they have three-part bodies: head, thorax, and abdomen.

The head contains a pair of antennae, eyes, and the proboscis.

Antennae, used to smell, taste, and touch, function as highly sensitive "noses" and "fingers" for these insects.

Butterflies don't have long-distance vision, as birds and mammals do. Unlike human eyes, their compound eyes can't move or keep an object in focus. Instead, compound eyes see an image, made up of thousands of smaller images. They can distinguish shapes, patterns, and nearby movements. These insects also have good color vision, and are drawn to the color red.

▶ An Atlas moth from Malaysia is a heavyweight among moths. Those fringed antennae can pick up very faint and faraway scents.

KEY DIFFERENCES	
MOST BUTTERFLIES	MOST MOTHS
Fly by day	Fly at night
Rest with wings upright	Stretch wings flat at rest
Antennae have knobs	Antennae are straight or feathery
Form a chrysalis	Form a cocoon

Butterflies and moths also have a pair of simple eyes, set above the compound eyes. These are sensitive to light, and influence how the compound eyes see.

They may be near-sighted, but some butterflies and many moths see things that human eyes cannot. With their ultraviolet vision, they see patterns on flowers and other butterflies. This helps them locate food and potential mates.

▼ Each wing is composed of tiny scales, magnified here.

Since butterflies have been on earth so long, parts of them have evolved over time. Long ago, they had mouth parts that could chew. As more flowering plants appeared on earth, the mouth parts of most species became long and hollow, to drink nectar. This hollow feeding tube, called a proboscis, works like a garden hose. It stays coiled below the butterfly's head until the insect uncoils it to drink.

The thorax or midsection anchors two sets of forewings and hindwings and three pairs of legs. All six legs are strong and have hooks at the tips to cling to a perch. Along with the antennae, the feet of a butterfly

may contain taste buds. When these species land on flowers with even a trace of sweetness, the proboscis rolls out like a party favor.

Both butterflies and moths have wings of all sizes, shapes, colors, and patterns. Moths are often thought of as dull and drab, but some species are more colorful than butterflies.

Most moths have a smooth, gliding flight. Butterflies, however, wander all over the place, darting here and there, stopping and back-tracking. Some scientists think that this random-looking flight pattern developed to fool predators.

The body of a medium-sized butterfly weighs about the same as a large bee, but its wings are about 20 times larger than those of a bee. The forewings carry the creature in flight. Without them, a butterfly can't lift off. Hindwings help glide, change speed, and steer. They may be torn or broken, but that won't ground the flight.

Wing scales overlap to create abundant colors and patterns. Scales also add strength to the wings and aid flight. Veins stiffen the wing further. Butterfly wings are so gorgeous, it's tempting to touch them. But even a gentle touch knocks off thousands of scales, which turn to powdery dust. Without scales, a butterfly may lose its ability to fly, and its life.

Some of its rich colors come from pigment. Scales can be pigmented red, yellow, orange, black, gray, brown, or black. When butterflies and moths wear vivid greens, blues, and violets, those colors come from a neat trick called iridescence. (Scientists call them structural colors.)

They are produced by light hitting the thin layers of a butterfly's wing a certain way. The feathers of peacocks and hummingbirds use iridescence, too.

The blue morpho butterfly found in the Amazon rainforest shimmers with iridescent color. A typical morpho has 15 square inches of wing surface. On each square inch are 165 rows of scales, with 600 scales in each row, totaling 99,000 scales. That means that the wings of a single morpho butterfly hold nearly 1.5 million scales! At times, the morpho needs to hide its flashy colors from predators. So the undersides of its wings are brown, blending with the tree bark it rests upon.

A few butterflies known as glasswings are transparent. These dainty see-throughs of Central and South America become nearly invisible as they rest on the rainforest floor or hide against vegetation.

The abdomen of butterflies and moths is also covered by scales, as well as hairs. In moths, some of these scales are modified to release scent. The abdomen also carries the digestive system, reproductive organs, and scent organs.

▶ Rainforest habitat, with its wealth of trees and plants, is home to huge numbers of moths and butterflies. This forest rich with tree ferns is in the West Indies.

◄ The sunset moth of Madagascar Island has large iridescent wings. The fringed tails on the edges of its wings help spread scent to attract a mate.

▼ A blue morpho butterfly of South America shimmers with iridescent colors on its upper wings. At rest, dull brown underwings hide its flashy topside.

From courtship to caterpillars

▼ In an Asian rainforest, two pairs of palm king butterflies (four in all) meet and mate on the same palm branch. Most butterflies mate on plants rather than in the air. The eyespots on their wings serve to confuse their enemies.

The life of an adult butterfly can be as short as one week or nearly as long as a year, depending on species. The longest lived may be the mourning cloak, at eleven months. But the typical life span lasts just two weeks. Butterflies need to find mates and produce offspring quickly.

The male butterfly begins his search as soon as possible. Some males have scales or hairy fringe that scatters a scent to attract females.

With moths, it is the female that releases scent, from glands in her abdomen. The feathery antennae of a male moth can pick up her perfume several miles away, and track it to the source.

◄ In the race to reproduce, butterflies must find mates fast. Courtship is brief, but can include chases, caresses, scent exchange, and dances. Here, a male hovers over his mate, a Japanese kite butterfly, in their courtship dance.

The brilliant colors and patterns of butterflies and moths are part of the mating game. These insects also perform courtship flights and "dances" before mating. Males flutter and swoop, and the two chase each other. If a female butterfly wants to say "No," she does a rejection dance, zipping straight up and down in the air.

If she says, "Yes," the two insects land on a plant, exchanging scent and touching each other with their antennae. Mating can last up to several hours.

▶ Eggs of butterflies and moths come in many shapes, sizes, and colors. These smooth, round eggs are from a northern pearly eye butterfly in Michigan.

After mating, a female butterfly may lay several dozen eggs or as many as 1,500. She often flies many miles to find the right place to leave them. Using sensors on her feet and antennae, she chooses specific plants to serve as food after her eggs hatch into caterpillars.

A few butterfly mothers aren't that choosy. The fritillary butterfly drops her eggs at random while flying. Moths also give their eggs protective cover but choose from a wider variety of host plants for their eggs.

The female lays eggs on the underside of leaves, stems, or flowers. There they stand a chance of escaping sun, rain, and predators. Fluid released with the eggs helps glue them in place and may protect them from drying out.

▶ After mating, the female butterfly searches for the right plant to serve as food for the caterpillars that will emerge from her eggs. This pierid butterfly deposits yellow eggs like grains of rice onto a leaf in the Costa Rican rainforest.

◄ The eggs of the palm king butterfly hint at what the adult butterflies will one day look like.

Eggs differ from species to species. They can be laid in a large group, in small clusters, or singly. One European moth lays eggs in a ring around a twig. Eggs can be round or shaped like a cone, dome, spindle, or turban. Many have patterned ridges. Most newly laid eggs appear as pale white, yellow, or green. As they develop, the eggs darken, often taking on patterns and colors of the soon-to-be caterpillar.

An egg can hatch in as little as two days or take as long as a year. The usual time is five to seven days. The new caterpillar—sometimes called a larva by scientists—chews a hole, wiggles out, and eats its eggshell, which contains nutrients for its growth.

Caterpillars bear no resemblance to the graceful butterflies or moths they will become. The head has a pair of simple eyes, short antennae, and strong jaws with cutting edges to devour plants. The thorax has three sections, the abdomen ten.

There's no trace of future wings on an earthbound caterpillar, either. Instead, multiple pairs of legs and over 1,000 muscles help it ripple along. The first three pairs grab leaves or other food while feeding. The other legs have stiff hooks on the end

► This caterpillar lives in the Costa Rican rainforest. To ward off big hungry birds, it puffs itself up to look like a snake. But its worst enemies may well be the tiniest: the white eggs on its face were laid by a parasitic fly. When they hatch into larvae, the caterpillar becomes their breakfast.

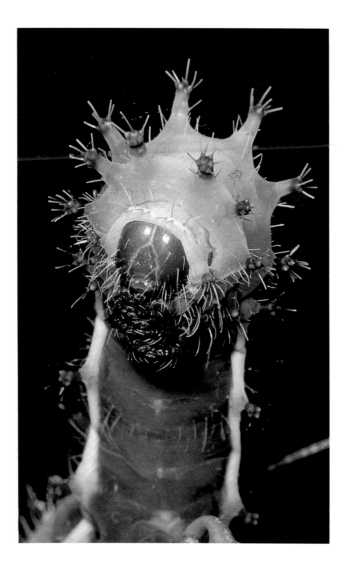

▲ In Australia, the colorful caterpillar of a gum emperor moth uses its dark mouth parts to grasp its food.

called crotchets. As the flat end of each foot contacts a smooth surface, the center draws up, creating a suction-cup effect.

Right away, the tiny caterpillar or larva begins to eat plant leaves. It eats. And eats. And eats. In one day, it may gobble twice its weight in food. In fact, it may grow to nearly 1,000 times its original weight.

How does its body deal with so much growth? Instead of having a skeleton inside, the caterpillar wears a thin, cellophane-like outer covering called an exoskeleton. When stretched to the limit, the exoskeleton splits. The caterpillar stops eating, spins a silk pad to anchor its legs, and begins to shrug off its exoskeleton, like a pair of too-tight jeans. A new, more comfortable exoskeleton lies just beneath the old one. This process, known as molting, happens four or five times in a caterpillar's life. Each time it molts, the caterpillar nearly doubles in size.

Caterpillars come in as many colors and shapes as butterflies and moths do. This variety helps them hide from a long list of predators: birds, frogs, lizards, wasps, ants, and small mammals. To keep enemies guessing, they may look different after each molt.

Among their disguises: markings that look like a snake, a dead leaf, or even bird droppings. One caterpillar might wear whip-like tails, horns, or poisonous spines. Another might have bad-smelling tentacles growing out of its body to discourage birds. The caterpillar of the woolly bear moth has a furry coat that can cause allergic reactions. Its coat also keeps smaller insects from laying parasitic eggs on it.

Some caterpillars deliberately feed on poisonous plants, then hold the toxins in their system. To warn off snackers, they advertise with bright colors of pink, green, yellow, red, or orange, decorated with spots or stripes. The caterpillar of the cabbage butterfly carries poison droplets on its back. Any ant unlucky enough to run into this larva backs away and starts detox operations.

Other caterpillars form partnerships with ants. These symbiotic relationships occur between some species of caterpillars and certain ants with a taste for sweets.

In the mountainous forests of Mexico, for instance, a caterpillar from the metal mark butterfly family interacts with carpenter ants. While the caterpillar feeds at night on the croton plant, ants protect it from wasps and robber ants. In return, the carpenter ants receive honeydew from a gland on the caterpillar's back. During the day, ants coax the caterpillar off the croton into a small underground chamber they dig at the base of the plant. Sealed inside, it is protected from enemies.

In Europe and Asia, the caterpillar of a group of butterflies known as blues actually relies on ants for survival. In return for the caterpillar's sweet honeydew, the ants carry it into their nest. Because the caterpillar looks like the ant young and uses similar begging behavior, it is fed by adult ants. Without their help, it is likely the caterpillar would starve.

Some caterpillars, especially of moths, destroy crops, forests, clothing, and stored grain. The greatest damage occurs when a species is introduced into a new area. Without its natural predators and parasites, the caterpillar population soars. An example in modern times is the caterpillar for the Asian gypsy moth, which has destroyed millions of acres of forest on several continents. On the other hand, the caterpillars of the silk moth have been of great benefit to humankind.

▶ A startling false eye on its back may give the caterpillar of the Malaysian cyclops hawk moth a chance to escape from a bird that misses its real head.

The great change: metamorphosis

▲ LEFT: The caterpillar of a North American monarch butterfly eats milkweed, storing fat for its transformation into a butterfly.

RIGHT: The same caterpillar now goes into the pupal stage. It hangs from a branch, molting a last time and forming a new covering for itself.

Caterpillars go through about five molting stages, called instars. Each time, the caterpillar gets chubbier. At last it's ready for its final transformation, called metamorphosis— a fancy word for going from one form to a very different one.

Butterflies have a somewhat different metamorphosis than moths do. To start, the caterpillar of a butterfly spins a small pad of silk onto a leaf or twig, grabbing it with a hook on the end of its abdomen. Its outer covering splits and is shed for the last

◄When finished, the caterpillar, now a pupa, rests snugly inside a hardened case called the chrysalis.

time. The new outer skin hardens and forms an often-beautiful casing called a chrysalis. The caterpillar now becomes a pupa.

The moth caterpillar goes about things in its own way. First, it makes a cocoon, spinning it from silk glands in its mouth. Some caterpillars spin a heavy coat of silk; others use a thin silk cover. It stays in its cocoon until it emerges as a moth.

For both butterflies and moths, the pupal stage can last from a few days to a few years, depending on species. For most, it's two to three weeks. During this time,

hormones turn the basic structures inside the caterpillar into butterfly or moth parts.

Cocoons and chrysalises are often camouflaged to look like dried leaves, plant parts, or seeds. Snug inside, the transforming insect lives on its fat reserves stored up while a caterpillar. It does not eat, and barely moves. Air reaches it through breathing holes, called spiracles.

Suddenly the chrysalis shakes and splits open, signaling that metamorphosis is complete. First a head emerges. Then come the thorax, legs, wings, and abdomen.

Clinging to the chrysalis, the new butterfly or moth dries its wrinkled and damp wings, flexing them to pump blood through its veins. As blood moves through, the hollow veins harden to support the wings. It may take an hour—or as much as a day—before the creature can try out its brand-new wings.

A butterfly must sunbathe until its internal temperature reaches about 65 degrees Fahrenheit. Only then are its wing muscles able to fly properly. What do night-flying moths do, to make up for lack of the sun's warmth? They vibrate their wing muscles to generate enough heat for takeoff.

Weather affects a butterfly's ability to fly. In temperate regions, a dew-covered butterfly on a chilly morning in spring is temporarily grounded. Mountain and coastal species wait until mist or fog lifts before flight. In late afternoon they find shelter for the night. During storms they find refuge under rocks or plants.

In arctic areas butterflies travel no more than two feet above the ground to make use of the sun's warming rays reflected off the earth. Desert species are active near dawn or dusk when the air is warm, but stay sheltered during the heat of the day.

Crowded skies in tropical and other rainforests hold the largest number and variety of butterfly and moth species.

▲ Although the monarch pupa does not feed, it is busy inside, changing form. In a week or so, the chrysalis becomes transparent, showing the new butterfly within. When the chrysalis splits, the new monarch forces its way out.

► While waiting for its wings to dry, the brand-new butterfly clings to the broken chrysalis. As blood flows through its wings, they harden.

▶ Temperate forests
harbor many butterfly
species, like this American
copper butterfly. Coppers
live in forests from East Africa to North
America, and in the mountains of northern
Europe and New Zealand. Due to habitat
destruction, some species of coppers have
vanished from England and parts of Asia.

◄ Most species of blue butterflies can be found in the western United States. Covered with dew, this tailed blue butterfly must wait until its wings dry before flying.

Moist heat allows butterflies to be on the wing from before dawn until after dusk. When not feeding near a stream or cleared area, they usually find their way to the cooler levels of the rainforest, from the understory to the tops of trees.

Since butterflies lose their ability to fly at about 40 degrees Fahrenheit, they are forced to hibernate during cold weather in many regions of the world. Species have adapted to hibernate at different stages in their life cycles.

For instance, when fritillary butterfly eggs hatch, the new caterpillar goes directly into hibernation, without even a meal. Viceroy butterfly caterpillars grow until their third molt, then curl inside a leaf for winter protection. Full-grown swallowtail caterpillars extend the length of their stay as a pupa to last through winter. Even adult butterflies of some species seek out sheltered areas. There, they hang with wings tightly closed until the spring thaw begins.

With body systems nearly shut down during hibernation, this versatile insect can tolerate cold of –20 degrees Fahrenheit. A caterpillar can snooze in frozen ground or even in icy water. A pupa encased inside a chrysalis or cocoon can survive being buried in deep snow drifts.

When the weather warms, the life cycle of these hardy hibernators continues from where it was before the interruption.

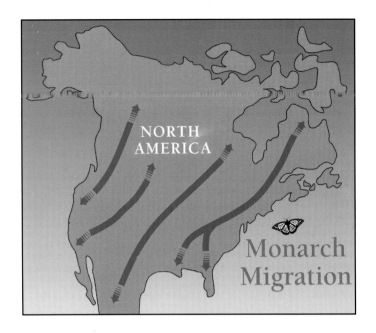

NORTH AMERICA

Monarch Migration

◀ Millions of monarch butterflies travel thousands of miles on their annual migrations, going from Canada south to the United States and Mexico.

How fast can butterflies fly? Pierids and blues mosey along at less than five miles per hour. The daggerwing of Costa Rica cruises at ten to 25 miles per hour. The giant skipper of Mexico holds the speed record, flying in bursts of speed up to 42 miles per hour.

But a butterfly's speed isn't as surprising as the distance it can travel. These fragile-looking insects migrate thousands of miles, some of them over open ocean. More than 200 butterfly species throughout the world have been known to migrate. By the millions, they do this. It's one of nature's most amazing feats.

When butterflies migrate, they don't do it at a flutter, as they do in a meadow or garden. For example, when the monarchs first head south to their wintering grounds in Mexico, they fly up into the air, looking for warm air thermals. When they find one, they ride it as high as 5,000 feet and begin to glide, holding their wings in a flat "V" pattern to save energy.

Why do they move? Migration seems to be triggered by conditions in their environment. Some species move with the seasons. Overpopulation starts other migrations, forcing adults to find new food sources for offspring. Still others migrate,

▶ Monarch butterflies spend the winter in a California eucalyptus grove. They hang in clusters on the trees, waiting for temperatures to warm to 55 degrees or more. Almost everywhere on its migrating paths, habitat for monarchs has dwindled sharply because of human development.

sadly, when their habitat is destroyed.

The spectacle of butterflies on migration is awesome. In Ceylon, a migration of three species of sulphur butterflies once went by at an estimated 26,000 butterflies per minute along a one-mile area. In Australia, the bogong moth migrates in huge numbers from the north to caves in southern mountains. Along the way in resting areas, moths cover walls of buildings and even stall factory machinery. In Africa, swarms of migrating butterflies crisscross the continent south of the Sahara. Cars often overheat when their radiators become clogged with masses of dead butterflies.

The painted lady butterflies found in Asia, Europe, Africa, and North America are champion migrators. In spring they fly north from Africa and the Middle East into Europe, even crossing the Alps. They venture into India, south along the west coast of Africa, and north to Iceland. In North America, one generation of painted lady butterflies leaves Mexico in spring, leaving the next generation to arrive in Canada and Newfoundland in late summer. During one three-day migration in California, an estimated three billion painted ladies flew across a 40-mile-wide area.

Another frequent flyer is the poster child of all butterflies, the orange-and-black monarch in North America. It migrates from as far north as Canada, going south to milder temperatures each winter. An estimated 100 million monarchs make the journey each year. They've been known to fly up to 100 miles a day and reach speeds of 30 mph, although typical flight speed is ten mph.

After more than a month of flying, all the monarchs west of the Rocky Mountains settle in California and Baja California. All of the Canadian monarchs east of the Rockies fly south to Florida, central Mexico, Central America, and Cuba. The monarchs arriving at wintering sites in Mexico number in the tens of millions. The numbers of monarchs overwintering in California is much smaller. Nevertheless, all of them choose sites that have fresh water and tall trees.

Before leaving Canada, monarchs fill up on nectar and store fat to use as energy during winter when flowers are scarce.

When it's cool at winter quarters, monarchs cluster together tightly on trees, each attached to a leaf by its gripper feet. They exist in a state of semi-hibernation until it's at least 55 degrees Fahrenheit and the sun warms their wings. Then they leave the tree to find water or to mate.

A female monarch doesn't lay eggs immediately but waits until late February. Just before the journey north, she lays up to 100 eggs on milkweed plants. The first generation of monarchs that migrated south now dies after living six to nine months. The second and third generations live six weeks each and then die. The fourth returns to Canada and produces the fifth generation, which completes the cycle by migrating south.

How do monarchs know to migrate and where to go? Through field research, scientists have discovered that butterflies such as the monarch use cues like the earth's magnetic field to find their way. They also believe that information passes from butterfly parent to offspring in a process called intergenerational memory.

Hiding out & passing for poisonous

◄Some wasps lay their eggs on caterpillars. They become parasites. After hatching, hungry wasp larvae feed on the caterpillar, soon killing it.

▼ Birds are big consumers of butterflies. In the jungles of Belize, a blue-crowned motmot begins its meal.

Both the hardy long-distance travelers and the butterfly stay-at-homes face continual danger from predators. Vertebrate hunters include birds, bats, mice, monkeys, lizards, frogs, fish, and small snakes. Invertebrate enemies include spiders, ants, beetles, dragonflies, scorpions, centipedes, and wasps. North American whitefaced hornets can even catch speedy butterflies like the American copper on the wing.

Despite all these creatures searching for an easy meal, butterflies manage to survive. Like caterpillars, they wear disguises.

◄Even though they hide, wear disguises, and are sometimes poisonous, butterflies, moths, and caterpillars are often eaten by predators. Their enemies include this nursery web spider that has snared a hairstreak butterfly in its web.

They also deceive predators with nearly flawless impersonations.

The monarch butterfly, which eats toxic milkweed as a caterpillar, retains the poison in its body, especially its wings. After sampling a monarch wing, birds as large as blue jays become ill, and small lizards can die. Once predators discover the toxicity, they leave monarchs alone.

The bright orange viceroy butterfly closely resembles the monarch. Beginning in the mid-1800s, Lepidopterists believed the viceroy was non-poisonous and that by impersonating the monarch it was left alone. However, studies show the viceroy has developed its own toxic defense, over the years. By continuing to share colors and markings, fewer monarchs and viceroys are

▼ The viceroy butterfly not only looks a lot like the monarch, it shares another trait. They are both poisonous.

sampled before predators learn to avoid them.

Aside from this famous pair, hundreds of edible species copy the colors and patterns of inedible species well enough to discourage predators. In some cases, along with duplicate colors, the impersonators copy the flight patterns of bad-tasting butterflies, too. This ability to copy another species is called mimicry.

The unpleasant-tasting pipevine swallowtail butterfly, found throughout much of the United States, attracts several mimics. One imitator is the red-spotted purple butterfly in the south. This colorful imitator, in fact, is related to the white admiral butterfly, a northern species, but the two related butterflies look completely different. Because no pipevine swallowtails live in the north, the white admiral has no example to mimic.

What about butterflies and moths that lack poisons or don't mimic others? Some have body parts resembling their environment closely enough to blend in. The king of camouflage is the Indian leaf butterfly in Southeast Asia. Its orange and blue upper wings attract attention from hungry birds. If it cannot outrun them, it does a disappearing act. When it lands in leaf litter and folds its wings over its back, it looks like just another dead leaf.

Butterflies have patches of color on the hindwings that sometimes look like large eyes. Biologists believe that these eye spots can startle a bird enough to allow an escape, or cause a bird to snatch a butterfly's hindwings where it will do less harm. Even with a bite out of the hindwing, the insect can still fly.

▲ Masters of disguise and shameless copycats, butterflies use camouflage while at rest to avoid being eaten. Thanks to its wings, this well-named autumn leaf butterfly turns into just another part of the rainforest floor.

▲ The wings of many moths, like this Imperial moth from the midwest, can mimic plants or tree bark. Since most moths are active at night, this mimicry lets them rest safely during daylight hours.

Although most butterflies roost separately, some species sleep in groups for extra protection. Clusters of poisonous butterflies give off strong odors to warn away enemies. Predators only need to sample one insect to know the rest are off-limits. Daggerwing butterflies in Costa Rica cluster together in the same place every night, all facing out. If one is disturbed and spreads its wings, a domino effect ripples through to alert the entire group.

Meals for moths & breakfasts for butterflies

Perching on a flower, a butterfly unrolls its long proboscis to sip nectar, deep within the flower's heart. Head and feet dusted with pollen, it flies to another flower to sip. In doing so, it helps plants reproduce, a process called pollination. Flowers that moths visit often have deep necks. Some moth species, especially in the tropics, have a proboscis nine to 14 inches long, in order to reach the nectar. Only bees pollinate better than butterflies and moths.

Most Lepidoptera species use nectar as their main source of energy. The best flowers produce nectar that has a sugar content of 20 to 25 percent. Certain tropical

butterflies, like the zebra longwing and the gulf fritillary, have evolved to eat pollen as well. By doing so, they spend more of their lifespan as adults, less as caterpillars.

Butterflies and moths also require nitrogen, salts, and amino acids for protein in their diet. Some flowers accommodate them by providing ten to 14 percent amino acids in the nectar. Other sources of protein include tree sap, juices of rotting fruit, wet soil, honeydew from aphids and other insects, carrion, and animal dung.

Male butterflies have a particular need for supplements. They bring a present to the female when they mate. Biologists call it a "nuptial gift." It's a packet of nutrients, sperm, and salts called a spermatophore. A male butterfly holds it in his body, and transfers it while mating. The packet may weigh half as much as the male butterfly. The female relies on the nutrients in it to nourish her eggs.

For that reason, most of the butterflies that gather at mud puddles, on stream banks, on damp ground after rain, or on salty or urine-soaked ground, are males. They may stay at these watering holes or "puddling clubs" for hours, soaking up extra nutrients.

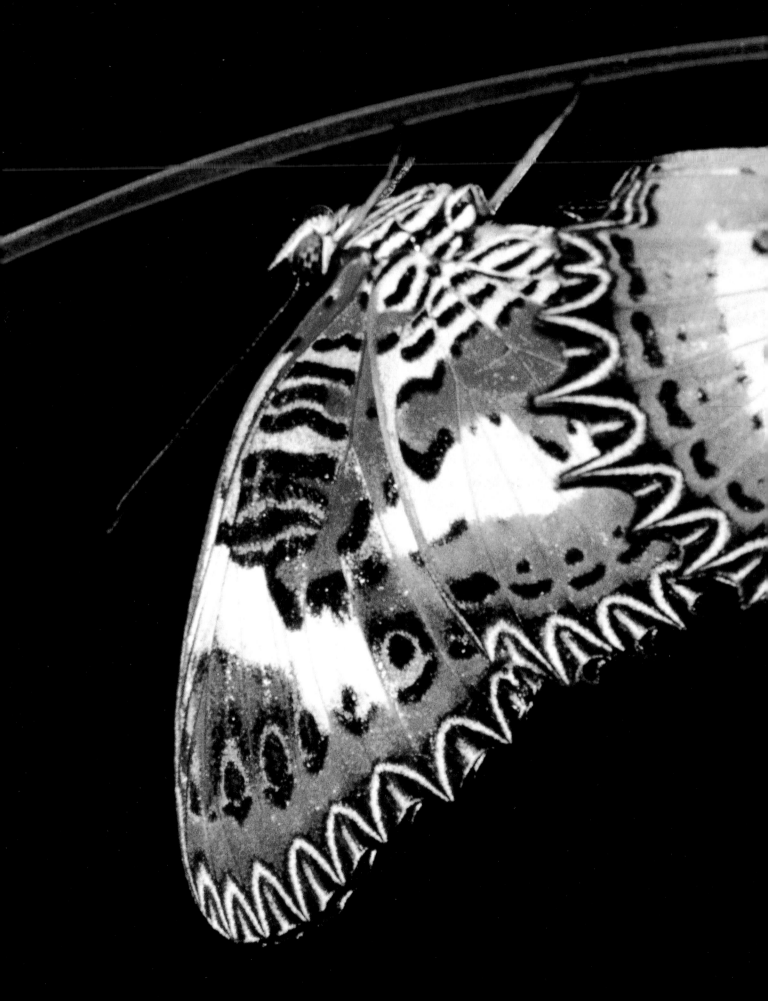

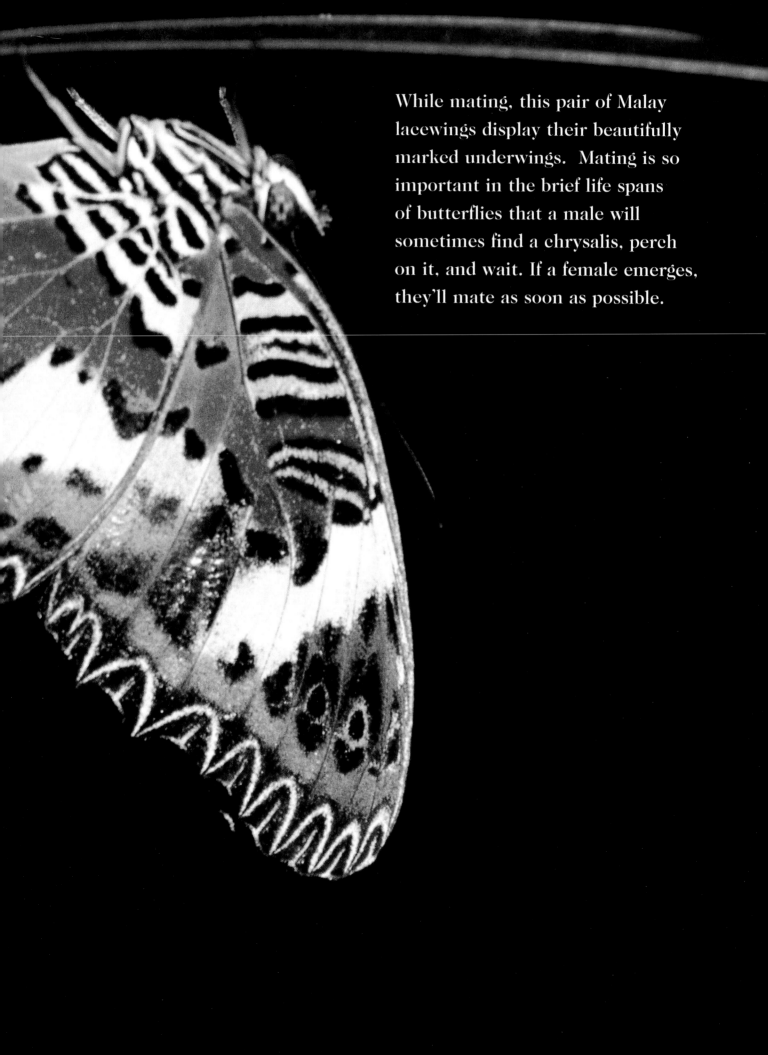

While mating, this pair of Malay lacewings display their beautifully marked underwings. Mating is so important in the brief life spans of butterflies that a male will sometimes find a chrysalis, perch on it, and wait. If a female emerges, they'll mate as soon as possible.

Ever since human beings have been on earth, we've marveled at these winged beauties, fluttering fearlessly about us. When ancient Egyptians built their tombs, they painted butterflies on the walls, to accompany them in the afterlife. To ancient Greeks and Romans, and to cultures from Japanese to Maori, butterflies represented immortality and the departed spirits of the dead.

A few centuries ago, attitudes changed. Butterflies and moths, especially large and rare ones, were hunted as trophies by collectors. Or made into brooches for fashionable ladies.

Today we appreciate butterflies and moths as living beings, for their beauty and their value as pollinators. Many nations now forbid or control the collection of dwindling species, like the paradise birdwing of Papua New Guinea and the homerus swallowtail of Jamaica. Like bird-watching, butterfly watching has become a passion for growing numbers who want to see these tiny dancers alive and thriving.

Like other species on this crowded planet, however, their future is threatened. Hundreds—perhaps thousands—of butterfly and moth species may face extinction.

How? Through habitat destruction, global warming, pollution, and overuse of pesticides. We see it in the runaway burning of tropical rainforests, a prime habitat for butterflies and moths, and in the draining and polluting of wetlands, another prime habitat. We see it in the way that human beings alter the landscape.

Some butterflies and moths have adapted to human interference. Most, however, cannot. Some species are gone forever, like the large Copper butterfly of the British Isles. In California, the Xerces Blue butterfly disappeared in 1941, when urban development eliminated its San Francisco habitat.

A recent development to save butterfly and moth populations has been the butterfly farm. Now located in countries throughout the world, these farms breed many species for zoos, collectors, and butterfly houses. Most farms are set up in the tropics, where they provide income for local residents and educate others about the sustainable use of native rainforests and species. Papua New Guinea has been a leader in protecting its rare species, at the same time funding butterfly farms run by local people.

Another positive trend: the explosive growth of butterfly gardens. Numbering in

► Newly emerged red lacewing butterflies in an Australian forest ready their wings for their first flight. While wings harden, they each cling to a broken chrysalis. When a butterfly glides, its wings flap slowly. When alarmed, the wings beat quickly, almost touching at top and bottom.

the hundreds worldwide, they vary from special habitats at wildlife refuges and natural history museums to commercial butterfly houses. We've also seen the establishment or restoration of protected reserves for butterflies, especially along migration routes. A good example is the Kern River preserve in central California.

Signs of human helpfulness are everywhere. July Fourth butterfly counts are held across the U.S.; Audubon field trips and butterfly walks take place in thousands of locales. Annual butterfly festivals around the world celebrate Lepidoptera.

Butterflies and moths are still present in our everyday lives. To make sure they remain there, it's up to us. That can begin in your own patch of garden. Providing habitat for butterflies is a small easy step with a big payoff.

In their brief lives, butterflies have much to accomplish. So do we. There is much work still to be done to save our planet, and wondrous creatures such as butterflies, from the threats they face. Thanks to the work of many caring people, there is still hope for the world's own symbol of hope.

▲ Pacific Grove, California, was one of the first towns to honor its population of overwintering monarch butterflies. It celebrates their fall arrival with an annual festival. Even in Pacific Grove, however, a growing population of human beings means that the monarchs lose more habitat.

Secrets of butterflies & moths

- A tiny caterpillar has multiple pairs of legs and one thousand muscles to help it move.

- Some moths, like the huge moon moth, don't eat or drink a thing during their lives. They live on fat they stored up as caterpillars.

- Many butterflies sip on urine, sweat, and slug slime. Others drink sap and rotting fruit. Sounds gross, but they need salts, proteins, and other nutrients not found in nectar.

- The mating of moths and butterflies is all about smell—but they have no noses. Instead, they catch scent with their antennae. A male silk moth can detect a female calling him at a distance of nearly three miles.

- One moth species dines on nothing but the liquid around the eyes of cattle.

- Moths, butterflies, and caterpillars are miniature masters of disguise. They can look like decaying leaves; bees; hummingbirds; or even bird droppings!

- To defend themselves, caterpillars shoot venom, wave smelly tentacles, and display poisonous spines.

- Butterflies can be speed demons. The giant skipper can fly in bursts up to 42 miles per hour!

- Because birds usually strike at a butterfly's head, some species wear eyespots and a fake head on their hindwings.

- Moths and butterflies are a pretty quiet bunch. But one species of butterfly makes a clicking noise as it flies. It's called the cracker or calico butterfly.

Glossary

Carrion. Dead or rotting meat.

Chrysalis. Hard outer covering of a butterfly caterpillar which protects it while the caterpillar undergoes metamorphosis inside.

Cocoon. Silky covering protecting a moth caterpillar during its change into a moth. It is spun as a coat of silk from glands in the mouth of a moth caterpillar.

Complete metamorphosis. The 4-stage development and change every butterfly and moth goes through: egg, larva (caterpillar), pupa, and adult.

Exoskeleton. Outer covering or skeleton outside the body, as insects have.

Honeydew. Sugary liquid, released by some insects, and used as food by others.

Instar. Name given to a caterpillar as it grows and repeatedly molts.

Invertebrate. Animal without a backbone, like a butterfly.

Larva (plural: larvae). Caterpillar of a butterfly or moth in the second stage of its growth.

Lepidoptera. Scientific name of butterflies and moths, meaning "scaly wing."

Mimicry. To copy or imitate; some butterfly species mimic a poisonous butterfly, to discourage predators.

Molt. To shed skin.

Nectar. Sweet liquid, containing up to 25% sugar, found in many flowers.

Pollen. Tiny yellow grains containing the male reproductive cells of flowers. When they link with the stigma of a flower, where the female cells are, fertilization takes place and the plant can reproduce.

Pollination. To carry pollen from one flower to another, as moths and butterflies frequently do. They are pollinators.

Predator. Insect or other animal that hunts others for food.

Prey. Insect or other animal that is hunted.

Proboscis. Long, hollow tube, used by most butterflies and moths to drink nectar and other liquids.

Puddling clubs. Groups of male butterflies that gather at puddles and other places to take in salts, minerals, and other things needed in their diet.

Pupa. Third stage of growth for a butterfly or moth. In the pupal stage, the insect does not feed and is sealed in a case called a chrysalis or cocoon.

Spiracles. Breathing holes on an insect or a chrysalis.

Thermals. Rising air currents, warmed by the earth. Some butterflies and moths use thermals to get to a good migrating altitude.

Ultraviolet. Describing light rays invisible to human beings but visible to butterflies and other creatures.

◄ Caterpillars have appetites bigger than teenagers. Here, caterpillars of the cup moth of India chomp away at a leaf.

EUROPE

About the author

Native Californian and nature book author **Joni Phelps Hunt** has written four books, including the National Science Teacher Award-Winning *Insects*. She lives in Central California.

Photographers

Sixteen superb photographers are represented on these pages. Principal photographers were Robert and Linda Mitchell. The cover photo of a Western tiger swallowtail is by Richard R. Hansen. The back cover photo of an Io moth caterpillar is by Alex Kerstitch. Stanley Breeden, pp 20,44; D. Cavagnaro/ DRK Photo, p.37 bottom; Hal Clason, p. 39; Michael Fogden/DRK Photo, pp 16-17, 19; Jeff Foott, pp 22 left & right, 23, 24, 43; John Gerlach/DRK Photo, p. 36; Richard R. Hansen, front cover, pp 31, 38; Alex Kerstitch, back cover, p. 12; Frans Lanting/Minden Pictures, p. 25; Robert & Linda Mitchell, pp 6, 9, 10 top, 14, 15, 18, 21, 32, 37 top, 40-41. Jeanette Sainz, p. 5; Kjell B. Sandved/Photo Researchers, p. 13 inset; Kevin Schafer & Martha Hill, pp 12-13, 35 top, 35 bottom; Larry Ulrich/DRK Photo, pp 4-5, 26-27; Larry West, pp 1, 16 inset, 26 inset, 28-29, 34; Belinda Wright/DRK Photo, pp 7, 10 bottom, 43 top.

Special thanks

- David Loring, SE Asia project leader, Dietrick Institute for Applied Insect Ecology
- Richard Hansen, wildlife photographer & biologist
- Julian Burgess, London Butterfly House
- Boyce Drummond, the Lepidopterists' Society
- Gary Dunn, Young Entomologists' Society (Y.E.S.)
- William D. Winter, the Lepidopterists' Society
- Julie Dahlen, Children's Librarian, Paso Robles Public Library

Where to see butterflies worldwide

- Many zoos, aquaria, natural history museums, observatories, arboreteums, and botanical gardens have butterfly aviaries or habitats from rainforest to desert, with a glorious array of interesting species in them.
- More than a hundred places in 32 states exhibit butterflies, ranging from elaborate facilities like the Los Angeles Insect Zoo and the Smithsonian Butterfly Habitat Garden, to the natural plantings and winged residents of the butterfly garden at South Carolina's Congaree Swamp National Monument and Alabama's Biophilia Nature Center. For details, go to: www.thebutterflyfarm.com/usa_public_butterfly_gardens.
- In other parts of the world: Europe has farms, parks, zoos, and butterfly centers, especially the U.K., including England, Ireland, Wales, Scotland, and the Isle of Wight. Denmark, France, and The Netherlands also have butterfly parks.
- Canada has butterfly worlds in Quebec, Alberta, Ontario, and British Columbia.
- In Central America and the Caribbean: Belize, Costa Rica, Aruba, Grand Cayman, St Martins have butterfly farms. In Asia and Australia, visit zoos, insect museums, and butterfly farms in Japan, Malaysia, and Queensland.
- Visit butterfly-friendly habitats within parks. Thousands of local, state and national wildlife preserves, wildlife refuges, and wetlands sanctuaries offer amazing open-air opportunities to see numerous butterfly species.
- Visit real rainforests. The nearest ones are located in Hawaii, Costa Rica, Mexico, Guatemala, Belize, and the Caribbean islands from Puerto Rico to Cuba. The money you spend as a visitor is a good way to encourage

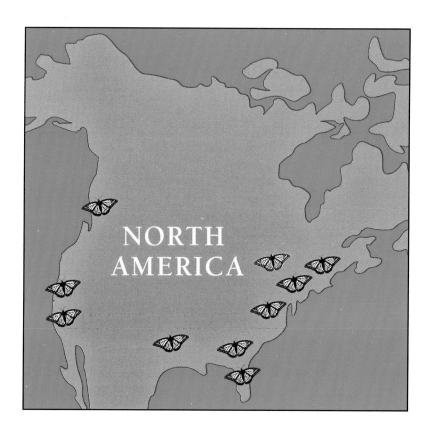

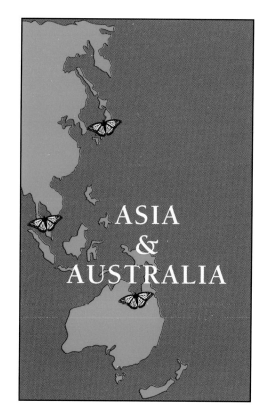

countries to save their rainforests instead of cutting them down.

- Go on real-life international scientific butterfly expeditions through Earthwatch International (www.earthwatch.org). It has programs for kids 16 and up; scholarships and teacher programs, too.
- Be a backyard butterfly explorer. Once you know where to look and what to look at, you'll be amazed at the different kinds of moths and butterflies you spot. Plant your own butterfly-friendly garden. Better yet, restore a butterfly habitat.
- Go see the seasonal migrations of butterflies. Monarch butterflies, painted ladies, and other species migrate. Their flyways and rest stops are well-known. Organizations like Audubon sponsor viewings and field trips. Check their websites for details.
- Take part in butterfly festivals. From California to Texas to the East coast, cities and towns hold celebrations in honor of their local butterfly species.
- Volunteer to count butterflies. Join in the nationwide butterfly count each July Fourth, sponsored by the North American Butterfly Association (NABA). See their website for details.

Helping organizations & good websites

- Xerces Society, 4828 SE Hawthorne Blvd, Portland OR 97215. Website: www.xerces.org
- North American Butterfly Association, 4 Delaware Rd, Morristown NJ 07960. www.naba.org
- Young Entomologists' Society (Y.E.S.), 6907 W. Grand River Ave, Lansing MI 48906.
- Audubon Society. www.audubon.org

- Earthwatch Institute, 3 Clock Tower Place, #100, Maynard MA 01754. Web: www.earthwatch.org

To learn more

Books & Magazines

- *Chasing Monarchs,* by Robert Michael Pyle. (Mariner Books 2001)
- *Handbook for Butterfly Watchers,* by Robert Michael Pyle. (Houghton-Mifflin 1992) Not new, but the gold standard by the dean of butterfly watching.
- *The Family Butterfly Book,* by Rich Mikula. (Storey Books 2000).
- *Golden Guide to Butterflies,* by Robert T. Mitchell and Herbert S. Zim. (St Martins Press 2001). Relaunch/ metamorphosis of a classic series. Great book for kids and adults.
- Print magazines include *North American Butterflies, National Wildlife Federation Magazine, Audubon, American Butterflies,* and *Insect World.* Online magazines worth reading: NationalGeographic.com has lots of butterfly coverage.

Videos

- "A Journey to Butterflies." VHS (2002).
- "On the Wings of the Monarch." VHS (2001)

Both of these videos focus on the monarch migration to the Monarch Butterfly Sanctuary in central Mexico.

Index

48